AMERICA'S SUPERNATURAL SECRETS ™

WEREWOLVES IN AMERICA

Colleen Ryckert Cook

rosen publishing's
rosen central®

NEW YORK

Published in 2012 by The Rosen Publishing Group, Inc.
29 East 21st Street, New York, NY 10010

Library of Congress Cataloging-in-Publication Data

Cook, Colleen Ryckert.
Werewolves in America/Colleen Ryckert Cook.—1st ed.
   p. cm.—(America's supernatural secrets)
Includes bibliographical references (p.   ) and index.
ISBN 978-1-4488-5533-9 (library binding)—
ISBN 978-1-4488-5582-7 (pbk.)—
ISBN 978-1-4488-5583-4 (6-pack)
1. Werewolves—United States. I. Title.
GR830.W4C656 2011
398.24'54—dc23

2011018010

Manufactured in the United States of America

CPSIA Compliance Information: Batch #W12YA: For further information, contact Rosen Publishing, New York, New York, at 1-800-237-9932.

Contents

Introduction

As long as humans have lived, they have shared tales of supernatural spirits. Indigenous people tell stories that are unique to their tribes but eerily similar to others told halfway around the world. Nearly all tell of humans and beasts linked by an unbreakable bond. In Europe, animal familiars—like a black cat—communicate with witches. Aztec guardian spirits exist within each person and can take animal form. African shamans go into a trance and turn into panthers. Native American wise men and women understand all living creatures so well they can shape-shift into coyotes, hawks, or whatever they choose.

It all sounds extremely cool, until the darker sides of these legends are shared. Details change depending upon which country the legend started in, but the basics are the same. When used for wrong, the power to shape-shift is an overwhelming, evil force.

Perhaps the most well-known is the werewolf. Sometimes the tale claims an innocent person was cursed by a demon. Hollywood has made lots of money playing up this story—an uncontrollable beast, transformed under a full moon, tearing apart or infecting others. The werewolf is a killer, but also a victim. It's not his fault. He can't help it.

Werewolves are the stuff of nightmares. A curse. A full moon. Man becomes monster. In an instant, an otherwise happy and kind person turns into a snarling beast out for blood. Nothing can stop it.

The real stories, though, are more complex. People wanted to transform. They used meditation or prayer. They smoked powerful herbs. They drank special brews. Sometimes they desired to connect with nature on a deeper level. Often people wanted to absorb an animal's powers, such as skill at hunting, stealth, or the ability to fly. Sometimes they wanted power to harm enemies. That's when they used darker means, including human sacrifices or deals with the devil.

People around the world believe they have seen werewolflike creatures. Could it be possible that some people turn into beasts, by choice or by curse? Read the following stories of werewolf sightings in the United States and decide for yourself.

Chapter 1

Sherman Ranch, Utah, 1994

The wolf appeared at the edge of the pasture while the Shermans were unloading furniture and boxes from the moving truck. The previous owners had left the 480-acre (1.94 hectares) ranch several years ago. The Sherman family bought their dream home at a bargain. They believed they were the luckiest folks on the planet.

A herd of cows was already corralled behind a sturdy fence several dozen yards away from the wolf. The family stopped moving and watched the wolf warily. All four Shermans said they were comfortable around wild animals. Besides, Mr. Sherman boasted, he and his teen son could easily handle the rifles and shotguns stored in the nearby pickup truck.

What happened in the next several minutes surprised them all. The wolf strolled right up to them. Its intelligent golden eyes seemed to mesmerize the family. They let the animal get close enough to nuzzle an outstretched hand. He was large, even for a wolf, and so friendly they assumed it must be a neighbor's pet. They took turns petting its coarse ruff.

The animal seemed playful. The family wasn't too worried when it moved closer to their penned-up cows. But then in a flash the wolf had a young calf's head in its mouth. It tried to pull the crying animal through the bars of the fence. Mr. Sherman snapped to action and grabbed his rifle. He fired two shots that he was sure had hit the wolf. The noise didn't even scare the animal.

The creature that wandered onto the Sherman family's ranch had golden eyes and coarse fur, like this real wild gray wolf. It was playful at first, they said, but then turned to attack a penned-up calf.

Mr. Sherman walked closer, still firing, and called for his son to bring another weapon. He fired again, this time with a powerful shotgun. He said he'd hit it for sure that time. He saw a large chunk of skin and fur fly off the wolf. Only then did it let go of the calf, but it didn't fall to the ground. It sprinted through the pasture and toward the river that ran alongside the property.

Guardian Spirits: The Nahual

Long ago, the great Aztec civilization believed in the *nahual*. This protector spirit was unique to each person. While a nahual could be a natural force, like lightning, most were animals. The Aztec believed a nahual could wander free while its human slept. Its human would dream whatever it saw. If a nahual was harmed, the same injury would happen to its human. People could interact with their nahual. They could send it to perform certain tasks. They could even take their nahual's shape.

The Aztecs died out, but their beliefs stayed among the remaining indigenous people. When some moved into North America's Southwest, they brought their tales of the nahual. In time it blended with Spanish shape-shifting legends and Native American skinwalker tales. Nowadays some consider the nahual a werewolflike creature that uses devil worship to transform.

Mr. Sherman and his son followed the paw tracks left in the muddy ground. They were surprised they couldn't find a blood trail. They kept tracking until the prints stopped in the middle of mud near the river. It was a huge leap from that spot to the water, one the Shermans said would have been impossible even for a large animal.

Where had the wolf gone? Why didn't the shotgun blast kill it? How could there not be splatters of blood on the ground? What kind of animal was this?

The many bolts installed by the previous owners inside the house now made sense. The windows were bolted shut. The front and back doors had several bolts each. Inside, the pantry and cabinets had bolts. There were large, heavy rings with heavy chains staked on either side of the house, as if for guard dogs.

The Shermans saw large, golden-eyed wolves several more times in the next months. Mr. Sherman patrolled his land with a shotgun and guard dogs.

A cow would go missing. He would find it dead days later. The poor animal would be gutted, with strange wounds the Shermans said looked more like a surgical site than an animal attack.

One time two wolves came toward Mrs. Sherman as she was latching the gate at the property's entrance. She climbed into her car to watch them. They paced near the fence, then one stood upright on its back legs. Mrs. Sherman said it stretched well over the top of the car.

Could the Shermans have come across skinwalkers? According to the Navajo, skinwalkers, or *yenaaldlooskii*, are evil creatures—humans who use the darkest of magic to transform into any animal they want. Sherman Ranch borders Native American reservation lands of the Ute and Navajo. These two groups share a long history of mistrust. Tales tell of killing and fighting. According to local stories, long ago the Utes accused the Navajo of releasing a yenaaldlooskii to hunt down and destroy the Utes.

The Navajo don't like to talk about skinwalkers. They are the purest form of evil, they say, created only to terrorize and destroy. To gain such power, legends say, a skinwalker must kill a blood relative. The skinwalker changes shape by putting on the skin or hide of the animal it wants to become. Sometimes, that animal is another human being.

According to the Navajo, skinwalkers dig up graves to eat the dead and steal their jewelry. Some believe skinwalkers can steal someone's body simply by locking eyes with that person. Others say the only way to avoid being stolen is to look the yenaaldlooskii right in the eye and show no fear. Many say talking about the yenaaldlooskii will get its attention and it will come after people who do so.

Those who do talk about their encounters share similar details, though. Multiple reports have come from outside Flagstaff, Sedona, Winslow, and Window Rock in Arizona. They describe an unusually tall, humanlike wild animal that runs incredibly fast. Some say they've seen it run on two legs

In Navajo lore, skinwalkers are shape-shifters who change their form by wearing the skin of an animal or even a person. Nayenezgani, pictured left, might wear animal skins like a skinwalker, but this deity fights evil.

The Sherman family had several encounters with unusual wolves. Their property was part of former Navajo territory, where legends say a skinwalker once roamed. Nowadays, the ranch is known as Skinwalker Ranch.

alongside cars traveling at highway speeds. A few say creatures attacked their cars.

Others have caught sight of one or more peering into their windows or trying to get into a fenced yard through a gate. They say a skinwalker knocked upon their windows, banged their walls, or climbed up on their roofs. Many

of these First Nations people believe skinwalkers exist, and this scares them.

The Shermans experienced other bizarre events besides strange wolves that couldn't be killed and seemed to disappear into thin air when chased. For two years the family endured sleepless nights. They lost several cows and two guard dogs. Their stories were so strange that they caught the attention of the privately funded National Institute for Discovery Science (NIDS).

The Shermans packed up their belongings and sold the ranch to NIDS in 1996. Paranormal researchers spent a few years trying to collect data using motion-sensor cameras and other recording devices. The findings were inconclusive.

NIDS shut down in 2004. Since then, researchers who weren't involved with the study say details from NIDS reports were inconsistent and questionable. Today, Sherman Ranch is known as Skinwalker Ranch. Bigelow Aerospace founder Robert Bigelow, a Las Vegas businessman who funded NIDS, still owns the property.

chapter 2

Werewolves in Wisconsin

Something strange has been going on in Wisconsin for many decades. Since the 1880s, people have reported seeing tall, fur-covered creatures with doglike muzzles and fangs. These creatures stand upright and move quickly. There have been so many sightings, and several in recent years, that Madison news station WMTV NBC-15 sent reporter Chris Pabst to investigate in late 2009. Here are some of the more famous claims.

Jefferson County, 1936–1972

One evening in 1936, a man named Mark Schackelman said he was driving along Highway 18 when he saw a hairy creature digging in an old Native America mound. Schackelman said the creature was covered in hair and smelled of rotten meat. Its face had both doglike and apelike features. Its hands looked strange, with a twisted thumb and only three fingers. When it stood upright, Schackelman said, it reached over 6 feet tall (1.8 meters).

Curious, Schackelman returned the next night. He saw the creature again. This time he heard it speak. The sound came out in a growl, with three syllables that sounded like "ga-DAR-a." Schackelman said at this point he backed away, praying the whole time. He didn't see it again.

There were no reported sightings for another twenty-eight years. Then one night in 1964, Dennis Fewless was returning home from work around

People in Wisconsin have reported seeing a huge doglike beast that stood on two legs. They say the creature stood over 6 feet (1.8 m) tall. One man claimed he heard it speak.

midnight when he had his own encounter. Fewless had just turned onto Highway 89 from Highway 14 when his headlights lit up an animal crossing the road. It was covered in dark brown fur. Fewless guessed it was about 7 to 8 feet tall (2.1 to 2.4 m) and weighed between 400 and 500 pounds (181–227 kilograms). He watched it jump a barbed-wire fence and disappear into the darkness. Shaken up, he drove home. The next day he returned to that spot to look for animal tracks, but the ground was too hard. He did see a section of a corn field where stalks were broken, as if they had been pushed aside.

Eight years later, a woman in rural Jefferson County called the police to report a large animal that had tried to break into her home. She told investigators that it had tried to get into the door but then left. A few weeks later she reported that it had returned. It tried to get into the house again. When it failed, the woman said, it went to her barn and attacked one of her horses. The horse suffered a gash from one shoulder to another. The woman said the creature had long, dark hair and stood about 8 feet tall (2.4 m), with claws on each hand. A footprint found at the scene measured more than a foot long (.3 m). Bigfoot investigators said they doubted the aggressive creature was the legendary Sasquatch.

Rock County, 2004

Strange creatures showed up in another part of Wisconsin in July 2004. Katie Zahn and several friends were hanging out in a field in rural Rock County. Two boys walked down a trail to shoot BB guns in the field. Zahn and the other two girls stayed near a tree, talking. Zahn noticed a huge clawed paw print in the muddy ground, much bigger than her hand.

Shortly afterward, the two boys came tearing down the path, yelling at the girls to get in the car. A tall creature burst through the brush. It was 7–8 feet tall (2.1–2.4 m), Zahn said, and covered in fur. She described it as curved and running on two wobbly legs. Its arms were longer than its legs, and it had a bushy tail.

Why Silver Bullets?

Legend says only a silver bullet can kill a werewolf. Why? Silver symbolizes purity and redemption in many religions and cultures. There may be a scientific reason, too. In ancient times, silver salts were used to disinfect water so people could drink it. Ingesting silver in small doses doesn't harm humans but does destroy bacteria and mold.

The teens ran back to their car. Once safe inside, they decided they had seen some mutated doglike creature. Urban legends claim strange mutant animals had been bred in secret laboratories and released in the wild. They drove to a bridge overlooking a stream, the site of another famous urban legend. There, Zahn says, she and her friends saw four more of the strange creatures. She told investigators the animals were kneeling at the stream and cupping their paws to bring water up to their mouths. They ran off when they spotted the teens. Zahn described them as having gold eyes and long, doglike muzzles.

Washington County, 2006

Two years later in Washington County, Steve Krueger was working at the Wisconsin Department of Natural Resources. Part of his job was to pick up animals killed along the road. He was filling

Sasquatch is perhaps the most famous American cryptid, or folklore creature. Many werewolf sightings sound similar to Bigfoot sightings. Could these creatures be the same? Could Bigfoot be a shape-shifter?

out paperwork in his truck one day after he'd picked up a deer carcass. That's when the truck started to shake. When he looked in his rearview mirror, he saw a big, hairy creature. He'd never seen anything like it. It had pointed ears. Its snout was bigger than a bear. He got out of there, fast. Later he filed an aggressive animal report with the sheriff's department. He described it as having a body like a bear but with a dog's face. It was between 6–7 feet tall (1.8–2.1 m).

Local news channel NBC-15 reported the encounter. They called it a Bigfoot sighting. Two young boys came forward shortly after to say they had seen a similar creature a few days before Krueger. They were jumping on a trampoline when the large, furry creature appeared at the edge of the nearby woods.

Where did these strange creatures come from? And why have there been so many sightings in Wisconsin? Krueger and Zahn both remain convinced they saw a creature unlike any they've ever seen before. Both insist it looked exactly as they described: unusually tall and covered in fur, with glowing eyes and long claws.

These stories seem unbelievable—overactive imaginations, many people say, or teenagers pulling a prank.

But several people in Elkhorn, Wisconsin, believe. They have seen similar creatures, too. In fact, so many people reported seeing a strange creature on a certain stretch of road that it became known as the Bray Road Beast.

Chapter 3

The Bray Road Beast

Lorianne Endrizzi was driving along Bray Road in Elkhorn, Wisconsin, one night in 1989. Her headlights caught sight of what she thought was a tall person standing on the side of the road. As she got closer, she said, she realized it wasn't a person. It was a creature covered with brownish-gray fur. Its doglike face had fangs. Its yellow eyes glowed.

Dairy farmer Scott Bray, whose family name was given to that stretch of road, reported he, too, had seen an unusual creature in 1989. He thought it was a dog, but it was bigger and taller than a German shepherd. The tracks he found were bigger than any dog or wolf tracks he'd ever seen. Russell Gest also had an encounter that year. He said the creature stood on its hind legs and slowly moved toward him. Gest ran away.

Heather Bowey lived near Bray Road. She was eleven years old in 1990 when, she said, she saw a large dog stand up on its hind legs and run off. Two years later, Scott Bray's wife, Tammy, saw the creature as she was driving along Bray Road.

All the people described the animal as being covered in dark brown fur, with pointed ears, glowing yellow eyes, and a doglike face. They all said the creature didn't look like any animal they'd ever seen before.

Was this a group hoax? Local reporter Linda Godfrey wasn't so sure. She investigated the sightings. She spoke with each person who reported seeing a strange creature. They all seemed sincere and scared. While nobody said it

Many people said they've seen a huge part-dog, part-ape creature along Bray Road near Elkhorn, Wisconsin. There have been so many sightings, in fact, that there are books and documentaries about the Bray Road Beast.

was a werewolf, they all said they had never seen any animal like this before.

Why would they lie about something that would only cause people to laugh at them?

Reported sightings dropped off until one Halloween night in 1999. Doristine Gipson was eighteen years old that October evening when she saw the beast. She was driving along Bray Road near Delavan, Wisconsin. She felt her front tire jump, as if she had hit something. She pulled over to see what it was. As she stepped out to check, she saw a large, hairy creature running toward her. She jumped back into her car and drove off, but not before the beast jumped onto the trunk of her car. It fell off and landed on the road. When she drove by the spot later, she saw a lump on the side of the road.

As people around town heard details of her story, more started to come forward. They said they, too, had spotted strange creatures lurking around trees or fields. They had seen strange glowing eyes on what seemed to be an unusually tall wild animal. Godfrey continued her research. She published a book, *The Bray Road Beast: Tailing Wisconsin's Werewolf*, in 2006.

This sketch by Linda Godfrey, author of *The Bray Road Beast*, is based on descriptions by several people. Some spotted the creature on the side of the road eating dead animals. Others saw it sprinting into the woods.

Sightings of creatures that couldn't be explained or recognized seemed to drop off until October 22, 2010. That's when twenty-two-year-old Christopher Wohlgefahrt and twenty-four-year-old Andy Vyvyan spotted two creatures walking in a muddy field just off Bray Road.

How Big Are Real Wolves?

Wolves come in different sizes depending upon where they live. In the United States, female gray wolves weigh 50–85 pounds (23–39 kg). They measure 4.5–6 feet (1.4–1.9 m) from nose to tail. Male gray wolves weigh 85–130 pounds (39–59 kg) and measure 5–6.5 feet (1.5–2 m). They stand 26–32 inches tall (66–81 centimeters). Wolves grow larger in colder regions.

Red wolves became extinct in the wild in 1980. Conservationists introduced a hybrid species of captured red wolves bred with coyotes. These females weigh 40–75 pounds (18–34 kg). Males weigh 50–85 pounds (23–39 kg). The average length from nose to tail is 4.5–5.5 feet (1.4–1.7 m). Red wolves stand about 26 inches (66 cm) tall.

The young men described the creatures as being around 7 feet tall (2.1 m). They both had pointed ears, long muzzles, and yellow eyes that seemed to glow in the night. Their arms looked long and slender. The creatures were walking on what Vyvyan and Wohlgefahrt called "three-jointed dog legs." Then both creatures dropped on all fours and sped off into the woods.

Could It Be a Werewolf?

For many years Linda Godfrey has studied the reports and talked to witnesses. Even now she gets several reports each week from people around the world who claim they have seen something similar to the Bray Road Beast.

Godfrey says she wonders if these creatures might be timber wolves. Maybe over time they adapted to move on their hind legs. At the same time, she notes, humans still don't know all the secrets of the world. Many theories come about from things scientists can't yet prove. We only see evidence of the existence of many things in our universe. As Godfrey puts it, human senses can't hear all sound waves out there or see all the light wavelengths.

Have humans already discovered all the remarkable things to see in this world? Are there more mysteries?

Chapter 4

Other Sightings Around the United States

People all over the United States have reported seeing strange, humanlike creatures. It hasn't just happened in Wisconsin or near reservation lands. Some think it might be Sasquatch. But crypto-zoologists—researchers who seek proof of creatures like Bigfoot and werewolves—make a specific distinction. They don't believe these creatures are aggressive. These sightings seem to suggest creatures who aren't afraid of people.

The Wolf Man of Defiance, Ohio

In the summer of 1973, many people in Defiance, Ohio, had encounters with a werewolflike creature. Newspaper reports told of a scary creature terrorizing the town. The first sighting happened in late July near the train tracks that ran along Fifth Street. According to reports, a tall creature covered in long hair came charging out of the woods. It swung a piece of wood at three railroad workers. Two ran off, but the third was injured.

The attack happened in the middle of the night. The railroad workers reported the incident to police. When asked to describe the attacker, the men were frightened. They all said it had the face of some kind of animal.

The newspaper picked up the story. In the next weeks, several others came forward. Many said they didn't actually see anything but believed

something was out there watching them. One woman reported that something had rattled her front doorknob several nights in a row. It always happened at 2:00 AM. Another person reported something scratching at her front door.

Those who did report a sighting said it was an unusually tall creature holding a club or large stick. Fur covered it, including its feet. Some said it wore blue jeans and a dark shirt. Others said they only saw fur. Sometimes it chased after people. All the sightings happened in the middle of the night. Most people who saw it said it was not human.

Police figured some robber liked to wear a costume and mask. They took the reports seriously because of the wounded railroad worker. For three weeks the people of Defiance called with sightings and claims. Then around mid-August the sightings stopped. If there have been other sightings since then, nobody's come forward.

Talbot County, Georgia, Circa 1850s

According to some believers, there's a werewolf buried in Talbot County, Georgia. But this supposed wolf man is actually a wolf woman.

Local tales tell of a time in the late 1850s when sheep were attacked and killed all over town. Based on the animal wounds, local farmers assumed it was a wolf. They set traps. They sent guards with guns to patrol at night, but they never could catch it in action.

There are a few versions of the story, depending on whom you talk to. In most versions, the farmers worked together to catch the wolf. The stories describe how on the night the posse set out, someone saw a small, dark shape lunge at a sheep. A shot rang out. Instead of an animal howl, the shooter heard what sounded like a woman's shriek.

People all over the United States have talked of huge doglike creatures that stood on their hind legs. Sometimes the creatures ran from them. Sometimes, people claim, they tried to get into their homes or cars.

Lycanthropy

Lycanthropy sometimes happens in people who suffer from mental illness. It isn't a disease by itself. Usually, people who think they are wolves suffer from what are called psychotic episodes. They see and hear things other people don't see or hear. They feel things on their body that aren't really there. People with lycanthropy might feel or even see fur growing, though it doesn't really happen. They might snarl or howl. They might walk on their hands and feet. They might lash out at people.

But these people are not werewolves. They don't physically change. Their facial bones don't become muzzles. They don't sprout fur.

Doctors hundreds of years ago kept records of patients with this condition. Were werewolf legends created because of people who had this mental illness? Or did werewolf legends cause some mentally ill people to act this way?

This detail remains consistent among all the stories: the next day, they all heard about a young woman from the town who had somehow, overnight, lost her hand.

That's the legend, passed around on Web sites and told in the dark at sleepovers all over Georgia. But this case is particularly interesting because it is based partly on facts. The Burt family was wealthy and well-known in Talbot County. Emily Isabella was one of the four Burt children. She was born on July 29, 1841. She was described as small, dark, and very shy, with bushy eyebrows. Supposedly her teeth were long and rather pointed. Reports say she suffered from bad headaches. She sometimes roamed the countryside at night. She liked to read paranormal stories. And family lore says when she heard men planned to capture the wolf, she got really upset.

The night the posse set out in search of the wolf, Emily Isabella also went out. Her mother, worried about her daughter, followed her. Like many women of that era, Mrs. Burt could easily handle rifles and guns. She followed Emily Isabella in the dark.

Again the story changes, depending upon who is telling the tale. In one version, Mrs. Burt saw Emily Isabella, knife in hand, attack a sheep. Worried that her daughter was a werewolf, Mrs. Burt shot at her. In another version, Mrs. Burt saw only a dark shape lunging toward a sheep and, worried for her daughter's safety, shot at what she thought was a dangerous animal.

Whatever really happened, all the stories agree that Emily Isabella was near the sheep that night and somehow was injured. The wound was so bad that she lost her hand.

Shortly afterward, Mrs. Burt sent her daughter overseas. Some believe Emily Isabella was sent to a French doctor who treated her for lycanthropy. People who suffer from lycanthropy believe they are wolves. The Burt family said Emily

In Talbot County, Georgia, locals tell stories about Emily Isabella Burt and her strange wolflike behavior. Did this young lady suffer from lycanthropy—a mental condition that made her believe she was a wolf?

Isabella was visiting relatives. Legend says the sheep attacks ended then. When Emily Isabella returned, more sheep were attacked. The attacks weren't as often, however. In time they stopped. Emily Isabella Burt lived in Talbot County in her family's home until her death in 1911.

We do know Emily Isabella was a real person. Was she a real werewolf? Did she suffer from lycanthropy and think she was a wolf? Was she the wild creature who kept attacking the farmers' sheep those many nights so long ago?

The Michigan Dog Man Film

It seemed to be the proof believers had hoped to find: an aged reel of film, packed in a box of junk bought at a Michigan estate sale in 2004. It looked decades old—flickering, spotty shots of children riding a 1970s snowmobile, a man tinkering under the hood of a '67 Ford truck, the family German shepherd.

And then you see it: a creature in the woods, covered in long fur. It's huge. It rises up like a man, walks a few steps, then drops to all fours and runs off. The person filming it and another man hop in a car and chase it down the road. The camera captures the creature moving among the tree line like a silverback gorilla. It pauses, turns, then bolts toward the truck with dangerous speed. It seems to be a huge dog, moving like a human. There is a close-up of terrifying fangs, then the camera falls to the ground, filming only twigs and shadows.

YouTube user QuinlanOUR12 first posted the film. He claimed experts said it appeared to be real, and it terrified them. Could this have been a werewolf attack caught on film?

No. It was a trick, although a really well-produced trick, by a man named Mike Agrusa. He played the parts of QuinlanOUR12, commenter Don Coyote, and tragic attack victim Aaron Gable. Agrusa used YouTube and other sites to show what he called "The Gable Film" and spread the Michigan Dog Man mystery. Posts about the film set paranormal discussion boards on fire. In 2010, Agrusa admitted he faked the film on the final episode of the television show *MonsterQuest*.

Other Strange Sightings

Mrs. Delbert Gregg was home alone one night in Greggton, Texas, in 1958. She said a shape-shifting creature clawed at her window screen. She told a reporter for *Fate* magazine that a huge wolflike creature had scratched at her bedroom window. She grabbed a flashlight and shone it out the window. She said as the wolf ran off, it changed into an extremely tall man. It disappeared in the darkness.

In 1970 in Gallup, New Mexico, four teens reported they had encountered a strange wolflike creature on the side of the road. The teenagers said the creature ran alongside their car. They increased their speed until they were traveling well over 60 miles (97 km) per hour. They creature, they said, kept up with them. One of the teens shot at the creature, and it ran off.

Every year people tell strange stories of doglike creatures that run as fast as cars and disappear in the dark. They talk of scratches on their doors, windows, and rooftops. And even in today's modern world, doctors treat patients who believe they sprout fur, turn into wolves, and go running wild in the night.

Chapter 5

Werewolves in Popular Culture

The werewolf legend is dramatic storytelling at its best. Hollywood has had lots of fun with it: an innocent, often noble person cursed by a terrible fate. In this story, the werewolf can't control the wild urges that happen every full moon. Scenes of stretching skin and bursting fur keep us on the edge of our seats. The chilling terror mesmerizes us when we read alone in our beds late at night.

But tales of people turning into wolves have been around much longer. The Greek historian Herodotus (born around 484 BCE, died around 425 BCE) was one of the first to write about shape-shifters. He talked of a tribe of shamans, called the Neuri. Once a year, each would turn into a wolf for what he called "a short season." This reflects the same tales told by native peoples around the world. In these cases, the ability to shape-shift is a gift that brings one closer to nature or the gods.

Then there is the Greek myth of a cruel king named Lycaon. The king didn't believe Zeus was an all-knowing god, so he tried to trick Zeus. He killed

Cruel King Lycaon served human flesh to Zeus as a trick. To punish him, Zeus turned him into part man, part wolf. The mental illness lycanthropy gets its name from this story.

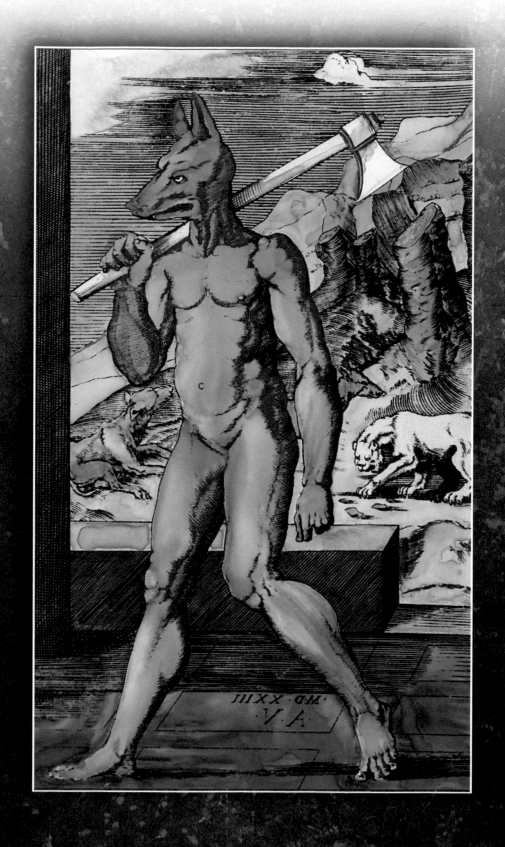

a person, possibly one of Zeus's children, and cooked and served the child as dinner. The story says Zeus was so angry that he transformed Lycaon into a wolf. This reflects the idea of a curse or punishment.

The werewolves of modern stories seem to blend different ideas of werewolves. Is it a curse or punishment? Is it a gift and honor?

Werewolves in the Written Word

J. K. Rowling's Harry Potter series features the heroic Professor Lupin. Lupin is an example of the noble, cursed werewolf. He was bitten by a werewolf as a child and forced to endure painful, horrifying transformations each full moon. He hides this part of himself in shame, but the scars on his body tell the awful story.

The pack of wolves in Maggie Stiefvater's Shiver series also must be bitten by a werewolf. The way they change, however, is different than Professor Lupin under a full moon. The shape-shifting happens with the changing weather. When temperatures turn colder, the werewolves turn into their animal form. When spring comes and the weather grows warmer, the wolves turn human again. Some seek out this life as a wolf so they can escape their real lives. Others, like the tragic hero, Sam, will do anything to avoid it.

Perhaps the most beloved shape-shifter in recent times is the Twilight series' Jacob Black. In the books, Jacob is a member of the Quileute. The Quileute are native people who live in the real La Push, Washington. Quileute folklore tells of how Dokibatt the Changer created the Quileutes from wolves. Author Stephenie Meyer tweaked that a bit. In her story, the transformation came about during a horrible vampire attack. A chief transformed into a wolf to protect his tribe. After

Harry Potter's teacher Remus Lupin (*third from left*) is a heroic werewolf. In Roman mythology, Remus and Romulus were twin sons of Mars who were raised by a shewolf.

the Cullen vampire family returns to Forks, the La Push Quileute youth find themselves transforming again. In this case, the ability to shape-shift is a gift for heroes.

The popular Animorphs series by K. A. Applegate is another example of hero shape-shifting. In this series of books, the five humans and one alien can change into any animal they want. They use this ability to fight off a secret alien invasion. Just a few more books with werewolves or shape-shifters include *Werewolf Rising* by R. L. LaFevers, Cassandra Claire's The Mortal Instruments series, and *Goosebumps: Werewolf of Fever Swamp*. There's even a guidebook for potential werewolves: *How to Be a Werewolf* by Serena Valentino.

Shifting Onscreen

The image of a man transforming into a werewolf is powerful. That's probably why so many people like movies and television shows about werewolves. The

Being Human

Modern moviemakers like to combine supernatural creatures. Popular films such as *Underworld* and the Twilight series tell of werewolves and vampires coexisting in the same world as the bitterest of enemies. The BBC's *Being Human* is a television show about what life is like when a vampire, a werewolf, and a ghost share an apartment. In that series, vampires and werewolves want to kill each other. In spite of that, vampire Mitchell and werewolf George have become the closest of friends, along with their roommate, a ghost named Annie. It was so popular that the SyFy Channel created an American version. In the American version, vampire Aidan and werewolf Josh share an apartment with ghost Sally.

very first movie about a werewolf came out in 1913. *The Werewolf* was a silent move that lasted only eighteen minutes. It was about a Navajo witch and her shape-shifting daughter. The filmmakers used real wolves in the transformation scenes.

David Naughton played David, an American tourist mauled by a werewolf, in *An American Werewolf in London.* **The 1981 movie had amazing special effects for the time, especially the scenes where he transformed into a wolf.**

35

At least six more movies were made between *The Werewolf* and the famous 1941 *The Wolf Man*. That film starred Lon Chaney Jr. It was the first to feature the idea of a full moon causing the transformation. In the 1948 comedy *Bud Abbott and Lou Costello Meet the Wolf Man*, the werewolf was a hero.

About a dozen more movies were made in the next decade. Some were meant to be fun, some truly frightening, and some were just plain ridiculous. The werewolf made a comeback in 1957's *I Was a Teenage Werewolf*. In this story, a mad scientist caused a teenaged Michael Landon to turn into a vicious beast. Twenty-eight years later, Michael J. Fox starred in *Teen Wolf*. This time, the furry teen became the star basketball player.

An American Werewolf in London was a popular 1981 movie about two American tourists who are attacked by a strange creature under a full moon. Two other werewolf movies hit theaters that year: *The Howling* and *Wolfen*. Two years later, Michael Jackson's mini-movie video for his hit song "Thriller" featured an amazing transformation scene. He used the same special effects team that worked on *An American Werewolf in London*.

Even the Scooby Doo gang was bit by the werewolf bug. In *Scooby Doo and the Reluctant Werewolf*, Shaggy becomes a wolf man. He must compete in a monster race to lift the curse.

Recently, movie makers combined werewolf legends with the fairy tale of Little Red Riding Hood. In *Red Riding Hood*, the heroine falls for a mysterious wood cutter. Could he be the man terrorizing the town in wolf form? The Lon Chaney Jr. classic was also remade: the 2010 version starred Benicio del Toro as the tragic Lawrence Talbot.

The idea of humans turning into animals has changed along with society. The earliest people tried to change to get closer to nature's power and spirits. When humans began to live closer together, they found themselves competing more often for land, food, and love. The idea of shape-shifting turned vengeful. A witch transformed into her familiar to curse an enemy. Skinwalkers punished those who they felt wronged them. As society became industrialized, the idea of turning into an animal became something to fear.

The animal within needed to be hidden away. And in modern times of video games, texting, and MP3s, we find ourselves liking the idea of a noble beast, a tragic hero, or a savage love interest.

In the summer of 2011, MTV introduced a new series, *Teen Wolf*, based loosely on the Michael J. Fox movie of the same name. In this television show, Scott McCall is the typical teen outsider who gets special powers after he's bitten by a wolf in the woods. Suddenly Scott can hear things nobody else can. His reflexes cause damage on the lacrosse field, making him a star but also making a few enemies. Scott scoffs when his best friend tells him he's turning into a werewolf. But as the full moon comes back around, Scott starts to lose control.

Whether werewolves are real doesn't matter. The stories we tell about shape-shifters reflect how we as humans feel about the natural world.

Glossary

Aztec The people of central Mexico whose civilization was at its height in the early sixteenth century.

canis lupin The scientific name for wolves.

cryptid A creature that some believe exists but that there is no scientific proof of.

curse A source or cause of evil; an appeal for something evil to happen to someone or something.

encounter To meet face-to-face.

familiar A supernatural spirit that takes animal form.

indigenous Originally from and often unique to a specific geographic region; native.

lore The entire collection of knowledge about a specific topic.

loup-garou A werewolf in legends from Canada and the upper northeastern United States.

lupinum The Latin word for wolf.

lycanthropy A mental illness that causes the sufferer to believe he or she is a wolf or werewolf.

myths Stories that aren't based on facts.

nahual A guardian spirit in legends of native Mexicans and Central Americans; also found in legends from the southwest United States.

Navajo A Native American people who now live on reservations in Arizona, New Mexico, and southeast Utah.

nayenezgani A Navajo deity that battles evil.

Neuri An ancient tribe of shamans who lived outside of ancient Scythia and became wolves for a short season.

Ojibwa Native American people who live west of Lake Superior; also called the Chippewa.

paranormal Describes an experience that science can't explain.

Sasquatch Another name for Bigfoot, a large, hairy humanlike creature said to live in the wilds of the United States and Canada.

shape-shifter A creature or thing that can change shape at will or that does so under certain conditions.

sighting Seeing something unexplainable.

skinwalker A person with the supernatural ability to turn into any kind of animal; an evil spirit.

terrorize To bully or scare with violent threats.

wer The Old Frisian, Old High German, and Old Saxon word for "man."

windigo A giant from Ojibwa lore who eats human flesh.

yenaaldlooskii The Navajo word for "skinwalker."

For More Information

International Wolf Center
1396 Highway 169
Ely, MN 55731-8129
(218) 365-4695
Web site: http://www.wolf.org
The International Wolf Center strives to ensure the survival of wolves around
the world. It teaches people about the relationship of wolves to wild
lands and how people play a role in the future of wolves and wild
places.

Northern Lights Wildlife
1745 Short Road
Golden, BC V0A 1H1
Canada
(250) 344-6798
(877) 377-WOLF (9653)
Web site: http://www.northernlightswildlife.com
Northern Lights Wildlife Wolf Center promotes wolf and bear conservation
in Canada. It offers teaching supplements, creates petitions on conservation topics, and posts news about wildlife issues.

Professor Cline's Haunted Monster Museum
Natural Bridge, VA 24578
(800) 533-1410
Web site: http://naturalbridgeva.com/haunted_museum_and_dinosaurs.htm
This haunted mansion features monsters and scary places. It's part of
Virginia's Natural Bridge Park. Stop by for scary and nonscary tours.

Society for Shamanic Practitioners
2300 Eighth Street
Olivenhain, CA 92024
(760) 586-8252
Web site: http://www.shamansociety.org
The Society for Shamanic Practitioners is a not-for-profit group dedicated to
     teaching others how the shaman goals of healing and health can be
     used in Western culture. It focuses on how shamanistic practices are
     being used in the modern world.

Wildlife Conservation Society
2300 Southern Boulevard
Bronx, NY 10460
(718) 220-5100
Web site: http://www.wcs.org
The Wildlife Conservation Society works to save wildlife and wild places
     around the world. Since 1895 the society has helped to save goril-
     las, tigers, wolverines, and whales and has started some of the world's
     most famous zoos.

Web Sites

Due to the changing nature of Internet links, Rosen Publishing has developed
an online list of Web sites related to the subject of this book. This site is
updated regularly. Please use this link to access the list:

http://www.rosenlinks.com/amss/wwlv

For Further Reading

Beaumont, Steve. *Drawing Werewolves and Other Gothic Ghouls*. New York, NY: PowerKids Press, 2011.

Dixon, Franklin. *Hardy Boys 59: Night of the Werewolf*. New York, NY: Grosset & Dunlap, 2005.

Feasey, Steve. *Changeling*. New York, NY: MacMillan Children's Books, 2009.

French, Jackie. *My Uncle the Werewolf*. Mankato, MN: Stone Arch Books, 2007.

Gee, Joshua. *Encyclopedia Horrifica: The Terrifying TRUTH! About Vampires, Ghosts, Monsters, and More*. New York, NY. Scholastic, 2007.

Hutton, Clare. *Midnight Howl* (Poison Apple). New York, NY: Scholastic Paperback, 2011.

Jones, Jen. *The Girl's Guide to Werewolves*. Mankato, MN: Capstone Press, 2011.

Kallen, Stuart. *Werewolves* (The Mysterious and Unknown). San Diego, CA: ReferencePoint Press, 2010.

Keck, Paul E, Harrison G. Pope, James I. Hudson, Susan L. McElroy, and Aaron R. Kulick. "Lycanthropy: Alive and Well in the Twentieth Century." *Psychological Medicine*, Volume 18, Issue 1; pp.113–120.

Krensky, Stephen. *Werewolves* (Monster Chronicles). Minneapolis, MN: Millbrook Press, 2006.

Oxlade, Chris. *The Mystery of Vampires and Werewolves*. Mankato, MN: Heinemann Library. 2008.

Pipe, Jim. *Werewolves* (Tales of Horror). New York, NY: Bearport Publishing, 2006.

Regan, Lisa. *Vampires, Werewolves & Zombies*. Santa Barbara, CA: Tangerine Press, 2009.

Rissman, Rebecca. *Werewolves* (Read Me! Mythical Creatures). Chicago, IL: Raintree, 2010.

Sautter, Aaron. *Werewolves*. Mankato, MN: Capstone Press, 2006.

Sinden, David, Matthew Morgan, and Guy McDonald. *Werewolf Versus Dragon* (Awfully Beastly Business). New York, NY: Aladdin, 2009.

Stine, R. L. *Werewolf of Fever Swamp*. New York, NY: Scholastic Paperback, 2009.

Toft, Di. *Wolven*. Somerset, England: The Chicken House, 2010.

Townsend, John. *Werewolf Attack!* New York, NY: Crabtree Publishing, 2008.

Troupe, Thomas Kingsley. *Legend of the Werewolf* (Legend Has It). Mankato, MN: Picture Window Books, 2010.

The Undead: Zombies, Vampires, Werewolves. Kent, England: TickTock Books, 2008.

Bibliography

Aldhouse-Green, Miranda, and Stephen Aldhouse-Green. *The Quest for the Shaman*. London, England: Thames & Hudson, 2005.

Animal Planet. "Lost Tapes: Skinwalkers." February 2009. Retrieved March 5, 2011 (http://animal.discovery.com/tv/lost-tapes/skinwalker).

Brightman, Robert A. "The Windigo in the Modern World." *Ethnohistory* 35:4; pp. 337–379. Duke University Press, Fall 1988.

Coast to Coast AM with George Noury. "Manwolf/Dogman Sightings." Aired January 2011. Retrieved March 5, 2011 (http://www.coastto-coastam.com/show/2011/01/07).

Cohen, Daniel. *Werewolves*. New York, NY: Cobblehill Books, 1996.

Godfrey, Linda S. *The Beast of Bray Road: Tailing Wisconsin's Werewolf*. Madison, WI: Prairie Oak Press, 2003.

Godfrey, Linda S. *Hunting the American Werewolf*. Madison, WI: Trails Media Group, 2006.

Guiley, Rosemary Ellen. *The Encyclopedia of Vampires, Werewolves, and Other Monsters*. New York, NY: Checkmark Books, 2005.

Hannity, Sean. "Beast of Bray Road." Video. FOXNews.com, December 22, 2009. Retrieved March 7, 2011 (http://video.foxnews.com/v/3935351/beast-of-bray-road).

Hastings, James, and John A. Selbie. *Encyclopedia of Religion and Ethics*. Whitefish, MT: Kessinger Publishing, 2003.

Haunted America Tours. "The American Werewolf." Retrieved March 2, 2011 (http://www.hauntedamericatours.com/vampires/WEREWOLF.html).

International Wolf Center. "Frequently Asked Questions About Wolves." April 2009. Retrieved March 3, 2011 (http://www.wolf.org/wolves/learn/basic/faqs/faq.asp#4).

Kelleher, Colm A., and George Knapp. *Hunt for the Skinwalker*. New York, NY: Paraview Pocket Books, 2005.

Ortega, Javier. "MonsterQuest: 'Gable Film' Mystery Solved." GhostTheory.com, March 25, 2010. Retrieved February 22, 2011 (http://www.ghosttheory.com/2010/03/25/monsterquest-gable-film-mystery-solved).

Papst, Chris. "Special Assignment: Wisconsin Werewolf." WMTV-NBC Channel 15, November 3, 2009. Retrieved March 5, 2011 (htttp://www.nbc15.com/news/headlines/70005732.html).

Roberts, Nancy. *Georgia Ghosts*. Winston-Salem, NC: John F. Blair Books, 1997.

Ruby, Robert H., and John Arthur Brown. *A Guide to the Indian Tribes of the Pacific Northwest*. Norman, OK: University of Oklahoma Press, 1992.

SkinwalkerRanch.org. "Hunting the Skinwalker Blog." September 20, 2010. Retrieved March 3, 2011 (http://skinwalkerranch.org/blog/index.php?/categories/2-Hunting-the-Skinwalker-Blog).

Spariosu, Mihai, and Dezso Benedek. *Ghosts, Vampires, and Werewolves: Eerie Tales from Transylvania*. New York, NY: Orchard Books, 1994.

Summers, Ken. "An American Werewolf in Defiance." October 12, 2008. Retrieved March 7, 2011 (http://moonspenders.blogspot.com/2008/10/american-werewolf-in-defiance.html).

Wisconsin Historical Society. "Effigy Mounds Culture." Retrieved March 7, 2011 (http://www.wisconsinhistory.org/turningpoints/tp-004/?action=more_essay).

Index

About the Author

The Wolf Man is the first scary movie Colleen Ryckert Cook can remember. Nowadays, she writes nonfiction for children, teens, and adults. She enjoys watching scary movies.

Photo Credits

Cover, p. 1 iStockphoto/Thinkstock.com; cover, backcover, interior background © www.istockphoto.com/Dusko Jovic; pp. 3, 7, 14, 19, 23, 30 (moon) © www.istockphoto.com/kycstudio, (silhouette) Shutterstock.com; pp. 5, 24 © Photos 12/Alamy; pp. 8, 15 Shutterstock.com; p. 10 Buyenlarge/Getty Images; pp. 12–13 Photo by Jerel Olson; p. 17 © Topham/Fortean/The Image Works; p. 20 Roberto A Sanchez/Vetta/Getty Images; p. 21 Drawing by Linda S. Godfrey that originally appeared in The Week, Delavan, Wis. Dec. 31, 1991. Copyright Linda S. Godfrey, reprinted with permission; p. 27 © denise roffe; p. 31 © 2003 Charles Walker/Topham/The Image Works; pp. 32–33 © Mary Evans/Ronald Grant/Everett Collection(10360474); p. 35 © Universal/Everett Collection.

Designer: Nicole Russo; Editor: Bethany Bryan;
Photo Researcher: Amy Feinberg